Introduction

"Nobody can do anything very much, really, alone."

Ursula le Guin

These questions are thought provoking and enjoyable. Ask them in the car, on a road trip or when you are relaxing. Ask these questions when you are both positive and open to connecting. Take the time to stare into each other's eyes for a full minute and then ask each other a few of these questions.

The more we get to know someone, the more we fall in love. You can get to know someone by sitting with them silently or going for a walk with them. Asking questions is another way of connecting. This is a way to get to know what drives your partner and discover what experiences have shaped them. By delving into our partner's thoughts and beliefs, we can better provide for them both physically and emotionally. Some of the questions are direct and deal in everyday concerns while others are more whimsical and aim to discover your partner's secret inner life. These questions are created to help you cherish your partner, if there are any questions you don't wish to answer, that is fine, the only real gifts are freely given.

Asking a question requires courage, while answering honestly demands faith. Without both, there can be no genuine understanding.

Questions are at the heart of being human and these are questions for the heart.

Question 1 – 111

Question 1

Where is home for you? Why?

Question 2

What is the best thing you can imagine?

Question 3

What do you hope to do by the time you are 90?

Question 4

Who is your family and why?

Question 5

Who was a great influence on you growing up?

Question 6

Are there any couples you aspire to be like?

Question 7

What do I do that makes you laugh?

Question 8

What is your relationship with money like?

Question 9

Do you need more space sometimes? How can I help to give it to you?

Question 10

Who has influenced your values the most in your life?

Question 11

Have you ever dreamed of riding a dragon or other imaginary creature? Which one? What was it like?

Question 12

What would your ideal job be if money were no consideration?

Question 13

Do you like who you are as a partner?

Question 14

What do you really enjoy indulging in?

Question 15

Do you need me to be there more? When would you like me there?

Question 16

What is the funniest thing we've seen together?

Question 17

When was the last time I hurt you?

Question 18

What is your first memory as a child?

Question 19

When do you feel valued?

Question 20

Would you like to start your own business? What kind?

Question 21

What are the three most important values to give to children?

Question 22

Do you have a favourite flower?

Question 23

What do you dream about?

Question 24

If you could invent something, what would it be?

Question 25

What makes you satisfied?

Question 26

Who would be the best people to raise our kids apart from us?

Question 27

Did you ever dream of going to the Olympics when you were a kid? What would you compete in?

Question 28

Who is your best friend?

Question 29

How would you like your life to be celebrated if you pass away?

Question 30

When do you feel like I'm not really listening to you? How can I hear what you have to say more?

Question 31

Have you ever imagined what it would be like to be an animal for a day? What kind? What did you get up to?

Question 32

Who cared for you during the school holidays?

Question 33

Do you like it when I run my hand down your palm?

Question 34

What is the best flavour for a pizza?

Question 35

What is the silliest thing I have ever bought that you know about?

Question 36

If you are unconscious and the doctors think there is nothing

happening in your mind, do you want to be kept alive?

Question 37

At what time of day do you enjoy sex the most?

Question 38

What do you regret?

Question 39

What is the most endearing thing I do?

Question 40

Do you have a favourite descriptive word?

Question 41

What is the worst thing that happened to you in school?

Question 42

Would you ever have an abortion?

Question 43

Would you like to be closer to our extended families? If so, how can we make it happen?

Question 44

What is your favourite cartoon character?

Question 45

Do you like being touched on the bottom?

Question 46

How do you feel about health care?

Question 47

Would we consider seeing a couple councillor if we need it, or even if we don't?

Question 48

How is your relationship with your father? Do you wish you were closer?

Question 49

What do I do that makes you feel loved?

Question 50

What would you do if our kid drank a chemical they shouldn't? Do you have a poisons hotline number on your phone?

Question 51

Are we eating well enough?

Question 52

Have you ever felt an affinity with an animal? Do you think it had a soul?

Question 53

Do you wish you had more siblings or less?

Question 54

Are you working too much or too little?

Question 55

What do we need to spend more time doing?

Question 56

Do you ever feel alone?

Question 57

What is the most irrational thing we've ever done?

Question 58

How should people treat the things they own?

Question 59

What do I do that makes you feel like crying?

Question 60

Who most often picks what show or movie we are going to watch?

Question 61

What do you feel like doing when you are happy?

Question 62

How financially secure were you growing up?

Question 63

Who in your family gives the best hugs?

Question 64

What do you really enjoy talking to me about?

Question 65

When did you last push your boundaries, what did you do?

Question 66

What is the saddest funeral you have ever been to?

Question 67

Are we getting enough exercise?

Question 68

Do you consider yourself to be a feminist?

Question 69

What would you like people to say about you when you're gone?

Question 70

What colours inspire you?

Question 71

Where is a new place you would like to have sex?

Question 72

Do you prefer the city or the country?

Question 73

What is the best thing that you have ever spent money on?

Question 74

What is freedom to you? Do you feel free?

Question 75

What is your favourite book?

Question 76

What is the most embarrassing moment of your life?

Question 77

How do we complement each other?

Question 78

What would you like me to call you when we have sex?

Question 79

What are some of the silly things I do that you find endearing?

Question 80

Would you like to spend more time with other couples?

Question 81

What was your favourite book as a kid?

Question 82

Is being happy a choice? Can people in severe pain choose to be happy?

Question 83

What is your favourite sweet food?

Question 84

What did you aspire to be when you were a kid?

Question 85

Do you have a favourite author? Why do you enjoy their writing so much?

Question 86

What is the warmest sounding word to you?

Question 87

How much income do we need to feel secure?

Question 88

Would you like kids? How many?

Question 89

How would you like to be cared for when you are sick?

Question 90

Who was your best friend in school?

Question 91

What is the riskiest thing you've ever done?

Question 92

Do we each do our fair share of chores around the house? How can we make it more fair?

Question 93

Would you like to get married, or do you enjoy being married?

Question 94

Who do you wish to be more like? Why?

Question 95

What have you learnt from failing in the past?

Question 96

What is your favourite time of year?

Question 97

What do you remember about the first time we held hands?

Question 98

Would you like to volunteer? Doing what?

Question 99

Do you ever feel lonely?

Question 100

What do you fantasise about?

Question 101

Is there anything you used to enjoy when you were younger that you would like to try again?

Question 102

What do you really enjoy talking to me about?

Question 103

If you die, would you like me to re-marry?

Question 104

When you are wrong is it hard to admit it?

Question 105

What other things would you like to experience together?

Question 106

Do you enjoy it when I am aroused in the morning?

Question 107

What things do I own that you would like to throw away?

Question 108

What was the last wild animal you saw? How did it make you feel?

Question 109

Do you sometimes say yes when you want to say no? How does it make you feel?

Question 110

When is sex boring?

Question 111

Would you like us to have a dog?

Question 111-222

Question 112

What can I do to make you laugh?

Question 113

What is one super expensive thing you would like to have?

Question 114

If we were pregnant and found out the baby would be disabled, would you want to keep it?

Question 115

Do you have a favourite genre of books or movies?

Question 116

When will our kids be old enough to have a serious conversation about racism?

Question 117

Do you think violence can be successfully opposed using peaceful resistance?

Question 118

What influence have your grandparents had on your lives?

Question 119

Would you like to do more for the community?

Question 120

Do you like surprises?

Question 121

Can you remember the first real intimacy between us?

Question 122

How does your love for me change over the time we've been together?

Question 123

When do you feel a bit down? How can I offer comfort?

Question 124

Do you wish you had more integrity?

Question 125

Is it better to be right or to make another person feel loved?

Question 126

What do you remember about becoming a teenager?

Question 127

Do you need to be alone sometimes?

Question 128

What is the best thing about being together?

Question 129

How can I avoid hurting you? How can I make it better when I do?

Question 130

Is beauty important? Will you consider me beautiful in twenty years?

Question 131

Do you think animals feel love?

Question 132

What did your parents teach you about being in a relationship?

Question 133

Is there something you would secretly like me to do for you?

Question 134

Should drugs be legal? Should smoking tobacco be legal? Should drinking be legal?

Question 135

Is it better for us to be comfortable or passionate together?

Question 136

What is the sexist thing I do?

Question 137

Would you like me to help you achieve any goals? Which ones?

Question 138

Do you quit when it is in your best interests, or only when you are

forced to?

Question 139

How do you feel about work right now? Do you feel respected?

Question 140

If you were going to give advice to another couple what would it

be?

Question 141

What is the best thing that happened to you in school?

Question 142

Where would you like to travel to that you have not been before?

Question 143

If you were single, how would your life be different?

Question 144

What is the best conversation we have ever had?

Question 145

Would you rather go to the beach or go shopping?

Question 146

How many times should we say "I love you," in a day?

Question 147

Where is your body the most sensitive?

Question 148

What other couple is most like us?

Question 149

Do you enjoy holding hands when we walk?

Question 150

Would you like more massages to relax?

Question 151

When are you creative?

Question 152

How do you feel when you write me a love letter?

Question 153

What would you like to do for our next anniversary?

Question 154

How will/ has parenting changed things?

Question 155

What is your favourite cake? Why?

Question 156

Do you make good financial decisions?

Question 157

What is the best thing we have ever done together? Why?

Question 158

What is the longest time we have ever gone without touching? How

did it feel?

Question 159

Do we have too much stuff?

Question 160

Should people live together before being married?

Question 161

Do you enjoy it when I brush your hair or run my fingers through

it?

Question 162

Would you like to go on a silent meditation retreat?

Question 163

Do you think trees are sentient?

Question 164

Can you remember our first date? How did you feel?

Question 165

Who is better at listening?

Question 166

What should I get you for your birthday?

Question 167

Should we hug more?

Question 168

How is your relationship with your mother?

Question 169

If we got pregnant, would you like to keep it a secret until after twelve weeks when it is safer or tell people straight away?

Question 170

Do you feel I listen to you?

Question 171

If you pass away in an accident, would you like your organs donated?

Question 172

What is your favourite thing about me?

Question 173

Where would you like to go on our next holiday?

Question 174

Do you miss me when we are apart?

Question 175

Where would you like to be in the next five years?

Question 176

Is it possible the earth is alive and thinks and feels?

Question 177

What are the best values your parents gave you?

Question 178

Do you believe in ghosts?

Question 179

What would you really like to buy that you know I wouldn't

approve of?

Question 180

Are you optimistic or pessimistic?

Question 181

When was the last time you felt I did not respect you? How can I be better at being respectful?

Question 182

How can we be healthier?

Question 183

What is the corniest thing that you have ever been obsessed with as a kid?

Question 184

What would you like to do if we ever consider getting divorced?

Question 185

Do you sleep well? Is there anything I can do to help you get a good night's sleep?

Question 186

What is the best smell in the world? Why?

Question 187

How do you feel when I get home?

Question 188

Are there any secrets we have that we wouldn't tell our friends?

Question 189

Who has the largest libido?

Question 190

Do you enjoy risk?

Question 191

What would happen if we swapped jobs for a day?

Question 192

What are you curious about?

Question 193

How would you feel if I was ever unfaithful?

Question 194

Who is your favourite among my friends and why?

Question 195

Would you forgive me if I ever made a big mistake in our relationship?

Question 196

What would happen if we got pregnant?

Question 197

What is your idea of success?

Question 198

Do you like it when I touch the back of your neck?

Question 199

Would you like to take a year off to travel?

Question 200

Have you ever felt like you didn't have enough money?

Question 201

What do you do that makes you feel good about yourself?

Question 202

Can long distance relationships work?

Question 203

How are we different as a couple than we would be as individuals?

Question 204

What would be our different parenting styles?

Question 205

Are there friends you would like us to visit?

Question 206

What can we do to be closer to each other?

Question 207

Do you like yourself?

Question 208

Where would you love to be proposed to, what is your ideal proposal?

Question 209

Is there something you do to arouse yourself?

Question 210

What do you do when I go away?

Question 211

Is being physically close to family important to you?

Question 212

What emotions do you struggle to control?

Question 213

Have you ever had a crush on a movie star? Who and why?

Question 214

What is the best thing about being together?

Question 215

Are you struggling with something at the moment? What can I do to help?

Question 216

Would you enjoy a breakfast date?

Question 217

When you come home after a long time away, how do you feel?

Question 218

Why did you ask me out or why did you say yes?

Question 219

Do you believe in one true love or fate?

Question 220

When have you been most stressed?

Question 221

How have you limited your own potential in the past by putting yourself down? How can I help you to be kind to yourself?

Question 222

What is your favourite song?

Question 222-333

Question 223

Who did you think you would grow up to be when you were a teenager? How is it different to who you want to be now?

Question 224

Have you ever been attracted to people of the same sex?

Question 225

Would you like to write a book? What would it be about?

Question 226

Are you comfortable telling me when I have food on my teeth?

Question 227

Do you have any spiritual or religious beliefs?

Question 228

Would you prefer to live somewhere warm or cold?

Question 229

How would you like me to dress?

Question 230

What does intimacy mean to you?

Question 231

Do you make wishes? Can you tell me one that has come true?

Question 232

What do you miss most about me when we are apart?

Question 234

Where is the most exciting place we have had sex?

Question 235

Is it important for one parent to stay at home when children are small?

Question 236

What inspires you?

Question 237

Would watching me masturbate turn you on?

Question 238

What is the next big purchase we should make together?

Question 239

How can we make our sex life even better?

Question 240

Could our relationship survive if your family cut off contact because of me?

Question 241

Are there areas in our life where we are too comfortable with each other?

Question 242

Can you remember the first time we kissed, what was it like?

Question 243

Have you ever loved an animal as though it were family?

Question 244

What would you like to do for Valentines' day?

Question 245

Do you feel like your family feels like you are a failure or a

success?

Question 246

If you were a superhero, who would you be?

Question 247

What are my three most annoying habits?

Question 248

Have you continued to do something simply because you did not

want to quit?

Question 249

What would you do if we had unlimited money?

Question 250

How would you describe our sex life?

Question 251

Is there a costume you would like me to wear when having sex?

Question 252

Do you ever feel like I blame you for things in our life?

Question 253

What is your ideal lunch time date?

Question 254

Do you need physical touch? How often do you need to be touched?

Question 255

How do you feel about your body?

Question 256

Have you ever felt unfulfilled with your life? What can we do about it?

Question 257

What is one thing we can do now to grow our future wealth?

Question 258

How are we different as a couple?

Question 259

Are you getting better at having relationships with people?

Question 260

Who would you like to invite around to dinner?

Question 261

How can we catch up with friends and family more?

Question 262

What is the silliest thing we've ever had an argument about?

Question 263

Which human being in history has had the greatest influence on how we live today?

Question 264

Are you comfortable with public displays of affection?

Question 265

What is the difference between routine sex and fantastic sex?

Question 266

Is it sometimes difficult to communicate your feelings? Which ones?

Question 267

Who initiates sex? Should I start it more?

Question 268

What really turns you on?

Question 269

Are you ok with how we spend our money? How would you like it to change?

Question 270

What were you going to do before we fell in love?

Question 271

Is there something that has happened to a relative that you are afraid will happen to you?

Question 272

What would we do if we won the lottery?

Question 273

Have you tried to break a bad habit? Would you like my support?

Question 274

What is your cultural heritage? Do you wish you knew more?

Question 275

Can you orgasm multiple times or simply once?

Question 276

What do you remember about the first time we touched?

Question 277

Will you still find me attractive if I gain weight?

Question 278

Who are you if you are not your work, your roles or what you look like?

Question 279

What are your relationships with your siblings like?

Question 280

Which animal are you most like?

Question 281

Could we survive if one of us fell in love with someone else? How do you feel about polygamy?

Question 282

What do you remember getting in trouble for as a child?

Question 283

Do you love yourself?

Question 284

What would you do if our daughter became pregnant when they are only a teenager themselves?

Question 285

Did you want anything different five years ago?

Question 286

When would you like to go to bed at night?

Question 287

Is there a particular position you really enjoy when we are having sex? Which one?

Question 288

What are our priorities in terms of where we live, do we want to change or fix anything about it?

Question 289

If you could be any animal in the world, what would it be?

Question 290

When was the last time you had a really great time?

Question 291

Who are your best mentors?

Question 292

Is it ok for a woman to propose?

Question 293

If either of us were unfaithful, would you want to know? Would our relationship survive? How would we get through it?

Question 294

What kind of gifts do you like?

Question 295

Would you like to design and build our dream home together? What would it be like?

Question 296

How important is sex? Could you live without it?

Question 297

Do you enjoy dancing? Can we find a song to listen to and dance right now?

Question 298

Is there anything you would like to not allow in our relationship?

Question 299

What is the best way to spend time together?

Question 300

Do you ever feel like a failure, when? Is there anything I can do to help?

Question 301

What are three sexual fantasies that you would not like to do in real life?

Question 302

What kind of car did your parents have growing up?

Question 303

If I had a new friend and you didn't like them, what would you do?

Question 304

How long could we last together, apart?

Question 305

Do you feel safe with me?

Question 306

What is your star sign? Does it reflect some of your traits?

Question 307

How much money would you like us to have?

Question 308

How often do we have sex each month? How often would you like us to?

Question 309

What if we tried to have a child and it didn't happen?

Question 310

When have you had the greatest load of responsibility?

Question 311

How well do you feel I express my feelings to you?

Question 312

Do you filter your water?

Question 313

What sports did you enjoy when you were a kid?

Question 314

Is there something that you are afraid of that has happened?

Question 315

When in your life were you terrified? What were you terrified of?

Question 316

If you didn't have to work, what would you do?

Question 317

What can I do to let you know you are loved?

Question 318

When did you first realise you had fallen in love? How did you know?

Question 319

What do you enjoy spending money on?

Question 320

How often do you climax when we have sex?

Question 321

What do you do when you are hurt?

Question 322

How will Artificial Intelligence change the world?

Question 323

Who are your four closest friends?

Question 324

How has our sex life become better?

Question 325

What were the most useful things you learned when you were a kid?

Question 326

If we lost a baby would you like to see them? How would you like to grieve?

Question 327

What was your favourite song when you were little?

Question 328

What is my most admirable trait?

Question 329

Do you ever feel like only you are responsible for earning money and does it weigh on you? Can I help share the load?

Question 330

When would you ideally like to get up in the morning?

Question 331

What is your favourite card game? Should we play more?

Question 332

What is the one thing I do that turns you on the most?

Question 333-444

Question 333

What is your ideal morning?

Question 334

How long does it take you to calm down after being upset? What can I do to help?

Question 335

Should parents discipline their children?

Question 336

Do you enjoy being kissed?

Question 337

Would you like to travel more?

Question 338

Do you wish your family were closer?

Question 339

What was your favourite nursery rhyme?

Question 340

Do you get sea sick if you travel on the water?

Question 341

How have we overcome challenges as a couple?

Question 342

What do you feel guilty about not doing?

Question 343

How do you feel about what happened during lockdown? How do you feel about the government and about how other people behaved?

Question 344

What was the first job you had?

Question 345

Do you feel better when our space is cleaner? Should we spend more time cleaning or get a cleaner?

Question 346

If we have a child, would you want them to go through religious ceremonies to be kind to our relatives, even if we don't hold those beliefs?

Question 347

What did I achieve that really turned you on?

Question 348

Do you prefer rainy weather or sunny weather? What is your favourite weather?

Question 349

What are you most grateful for?

Question 350

Do you like skinny dipping?

Question 351

What is the lowest point in your life?

Question 352

Were your pets important when you were a kid? Which pets did you have?

Question 353

What would you do if I was transgender?

Question 354

How would you cope if I died in an accident? What would you do? Should we write a will?

Question 355

What is your favourite texture?

Question 356

If you could go back in time and re-live one week of your life when would it be?

Question 357

What is your favourite part of my body?

Question 358

How would you like me to touch you? Is there a favourite place?

Question 359

Is there anything I wear that makes me more attractive to you?

Question 360

Should we bake our own fresh bread?

Question 361

Would you like to be famous?

Question 362

How do you talk about me to other people?

Question 363

Do you think we are succeeding?

Question 364

What is really important in life?

Question 365

Is there someone you know that you would like to befriend?

Question 366

What gives your life meaning?

Question 367

If you could make one wish, just for yourself, what would it be?

Question 368

What is our greatest ongoing expense?

Question 369

How do you feel after making love?

Question 370

What are your three greatest achievements?

Question 371

How do you help look after your friend's mental health?

Question 372

Do your hormones ever affect how you are feeling?

Question 373

What do you think makes you different from other people? What is

the same?

Question 374

If you could change one part of your body what would it be?

Question 375

Do you ever worry about an event before it happens and then enjoy

it when it does?

Question 376

Would we ever loan money to family?

Question 377

Do you look forward to holidays or dread them?

Question 378

If male contraception is available, should we consider it?

Question 379

Do you have a good relationship with your cousins?

Question 380

What drastic changes could we make to our lives to make them better?

Question 381

Do we need to socialise more?

Question 382

What small changes could we make to be healthier and have better relationships with other people?

Question 383

What is one thing that we can do now that will make our lives more fulfilling in thirty years?

Question 384

Do you meditate? Should we invest time in meditating?

Question 385

How can we be more flexible? Should we do more exercises?

Question 386

Do we eat too much take away? How can we eat healthier meals?

Question 387

What do you resent me for?

Question 388

Do you enjoy it when I get you a gift?

Question 389

Could we live with either of our parents if we needed to?

Question 390

What are some signs that you are angry or upset with me?

Question 391

Do you have a favourite pair of shoes?

Question 392

How do you feel about cars? Are you into them or can't you recognise one from another?

Question 393

Has the sex been getting better over time?

Question 395

Are you happy with how we get around? Do we need a new bike or car?

Question 396

Do you need to have a quiet day at home on some days?

Question 397

Is there anything I do that causes you to feel unloved?

Question 398

Do you need some quiet time after socialising?

Question 399

Do you like being shaved? Would you like me to shave you?

Question 400

When have you saved the most money?

Question 401

How do you feel about smoking?

Question 402

Do you enjoy it when I groom you?

Question 403

Would you want us to take care of the grandkids once a week when we retire?

Question 404

Do you prefer being warm or cold?

Question 405

How do you look after your mental health? How can I help you with it?

Question 406

Should we have an emergency fund?

Question 407

Do you feel less or more socially isolated after surviving lockdown?

Question 408

Does lube make sex more enjoyable for you?

Question 409

Are there certain outfits that you wear that make you feel more sexy?

Question 410

Do you enjoy shopping?

Question 411

When is it a good idea to go into debt?

Question 412

Are humans always more important than animals?

Question 413

How long could we survive another lockdown if a more deadly

pandemic happened?

Question 414

What do I do that turns you off?

Question 415

Would you risk your own life in an attempt to save someone else's?

Would being a parent make a difference?

Question 416

Do you enjoy it when I touch your toes?

Question 417

What did your parents cook for you when you were growing up?

Question 418

Do you consider yourself to be brave? What is the bravest thing you have ever done?

Question 419

Can you control your temper when you are angry? Have you ever been so angry that it has been a struggle? When, what happened?

Question 420

Do you enjoy cooking together?

Question 421

Have you ever been discriminated against? What happened? How did it make you feel?

Question 422

When did I last hurt you? What can I do to make it better?

Question 423

Do you think there is anything after death? Do you have relatives that are comforted by the thought that there is?

Question 424

Do you enjoy driving? Would you like me to drive more?

Question 425

Who takes longer to get ready?

Question 426

Would you ever kill for an ideal? Would you fight for your country?

Question 427

Do you have a favourite piece of furniture, that you just love?

Question 428

Have you ever been violent with another person?

Question 429

What is more important, snuggling or sex?

Question 430

Do you sleep better with or without me?

Question 431

Should we give more to charity? Would we give to a local charity or an international one?

Question 432

Do you enjoy watching sport? Which ones and when?

Question 433

Did you feel physically and emotionally safe growing up?

Question 434

Do you feel stressed financially?

Question 435

Would you like me to cut your hair?

Question 436

Did you ever overhear your parents arguing when you were younger? How did it make you feel?

Question 437

Were your parents good with money when you were growing up?

Question 438

Do you think the government should have to repeal one law every time it makes one?

Question 439

Are you more capable now than you were five years ago? In what ways?

Question 440

Do you think it's a good idea to follow your gut instinct?

Question 441

When do you want to sleep separately?

Question 442

What are you curious about right now?

Question 443

Do you sometimes move onto penetrative sex because the foreplay is not quite right?

Question 444-555

Question 444

Could you invite people over to dinner when you were growing up? Why or why not?

Question 445

Do you enjoy living?

Question 446

What is one experience that you disliked at the time, but made you stronger in hindsight?

Question 447

Have you ever been bullied? How did it make you feel?

Question 448

Would you ever consider getting an electric vehicle?

Question 449

Do you feel you have low confidence or high confidence compared to what you are capable of?

Question 450

What does being financially secure look like to you?

Question 451

Do you think adversity brings out the best in people?

Question 452

Are you superstitious? Would you walk under a ladder and do you delight in finding a four leaf clover?

Question 453

Were you ever abused as a child?

Question 454

Would you be a good grandparent?

Question 455

Do you look at reviews before you buy something?

Question 456

Would you still work if you could retire? What would you do if you didn't work?

Question 457

Do you enjoy playing with kids?

Question 458

How would you like me to initiate sex?

Question 459

Are you young at heart, middle aged or old?

Question 460

Do you enjoy clubbing or music festivals?

Question 461

Did you have a good relationship with your grandparents?

Question 462

Who can you rely on when you need something?

Question 463

What is the greatest source of conflict between us?

Question 464

Have you ever been to a gay pub?

Question 465

Touching which finger or part of your hand is the most arousing?

Question 466

Have you ever done drugs? What was it like if you have and would you do it again?

Question 467

Do you like chocolate? What is your favourite kind?

Question 468

What is our main aim as a couple?

Question 469

Do you check the weather before you plan anything?

Question 470

If you could only eat one type of food for the rest of your life, what
would it be?

Question 471

What is your favourite shape?

Question 472

Who are your people?

Question 473

If we have kids, in which ways do you want them to be like us and
in which ways would you like them to be different?

Question 474

Do you support a team? Which one? Do you want to watch them
play together?

Question 475

Where would you like us to have sex?

Question 476

Do you like the perfumes or deodorants I wear? Do you like my smell?

Question 477

What is your favourite sense and why?

Question 478

Would you like me to not wear underwear sometimes? Would it turn you on?

Question 479

How important is it to be generous?

Question 480

Do you feel you can trust me?

Question 481

If we have kids, how should we divide responsibilities? Would you help with feeding at night?

Question 482

What kind of complements do you enjoy?

Question 483

Would we let our kids sleep in our bed?

Question 484

Do you find it enjoyable when I do something for you? Do you enjoy doing things for me?

Question 485

Is it better to have a large population of people with an average quality of life or a smaller population of people with a better quality of life?

Question 486

How can I improve my communication with you?

Question 487

Do you think we see the same colours the same way?

Question 488

Who is better at arranging doctors appointments? Is there anything we need to see a doctor about right now like a skin check?

Question 489

Should we have a date night? How often should it be?

Question 490

Have you ever imagined getting old, do you prepare for it or have you always thought secretly that you'll die young?

Question 491

What would you like you happen if you ever lose your memory? How would you like to be treated?

Question 492

When is the last time you visited an older relative?

Question 493

What is a secret you have never told anyone else before?

Question 494

Would you kill an animal to eat it? Would you eat an animal already killed elsewhere instead?

Question 495

What would you like the courage to do? Can I lend it to you or prop you up so that you can finally do it?

Question 496

What did I do to win your heart at the start?

Question 497

Do you enjoy playing digital games? Which ones?

Question 498

Sometimes, does it feel like you're making the same mistakes? Which ones?

Question 499

Are there times when I'm missing out on easy brownie points with you? How can I get them?

Question 500

Do I have a tell when I'm not being completely honest?

Question 501

What is something you learned as a kid and never forgot?

Question 502

Do you think it's ok to dress pets up?

Question 503

Are you always prepared?

Question 504

As a couple, what is our Achilles heel?

Question 505

Which of us is late more often?

Question 506

Who cooks most of the meals? Would you like the one who doesn't to cook more?

Question 507

Do you ever want to touch my private place in a public place?

Question 508

What is the kindest thing a stranger has ever done for you?

Question 509

Are you ever in a bad mood and then realise it's because you went to bed too late, or haven't eaten? Does it help to know why?

Question 510

Who should do the washing up?

Question 511

If you had to pick two sexual fetishes, what would they be?

Question 512

Should couples share their finances or have separate accounts?

Question 513

What can I do to support you in your work?

Question 514

Should we have a package put together to take with us in an

emergency?

Question 515

Should one of us be the head of the household? Should we both be?

Question 516

Have you ever been sexually abused?

Question 517

Are there times when you would like to be touched non sexually?

When and how would you like to be touched?

Question 518

Do you think equality is possible?

Question 519

What is a something you can never resist?

Question 520

Do you like how you have to dress for work?

Question 521

Have you had a crush on anyone else lately? Can we use it to spice up our sex life?

Question 522

Which of us is the fastest thinker?

Question 523

Have you ever wanted to learn another language? Which ones?

Question 524

Should married people who are really unhappy with each other stay married?

Question 525

What is your dream honeymoon?

Question 526

Do you ever doubt yourself?

Question 527

What is your romantic ideal?

Question 528

Do you think life is harder for women than men or the other way around?

Question 529

When was the last time you felt I neglected you?

Question 530

What do you enjoy more, leading or being part of a team?

Question 531

Do you enjoy planning or do you do things at the last minute?

Question 532

What is the funniest thing I've ever done?

Question 533

Did you ever stand by while others were bullied at school? How

did it make you feel?

Question 534

Do you think what we feel is restricted by our ability to describe it?

Have you ever felt something you struggled to describe?

Question 535

Is there an extreme sport you would like to try?

Question 536

Have you visited other countries? How many? Which one was the most interesting?

Question 537

What is the most extraordinary thing you have ever seen that filled you with wonder?

Question 538

What kind of school would we send our children too?

Question 539

What do you think about commitment?

Question 540

Do you listen to any podcasts? Which ones and why?

Question 541

Can you roll your tongue?

Question 542

Have you ever had any nicknames? What were they?

Question 543

What would you like to be your legacy?

Question 544

When did you last lose patience with me?

Question 545

Do you think there is someone for everyone?

Question 546

Where would you like to retire to?

Question 547

Do you sometimes have to do things in your job that you are uncomfortable with? How can we change that?

Question 548

How did your parents talk to each other growing up? How would you like to be different?

Question 549

What is the most memorable present you got as a kid?

Question 550

Do you think we should make sure we have enough money before having children?

Question 551

Which of us has the better memory?

Question 552

Do you feel like I nag you? Do you feel like you have to nag me to get things done?

Question 553

What do you find endearing about me?

Question 554

If we were parents who would be the good guy and who would be

the bad guy?

Question 555-666

Question 555

How do you feel about childcare?

Question 556

Do you enjoy it when I rip your clothes off?

Question 557

What is your dream wedding?

Question 558

How did you feel when you were preparing for our first date?

Question 559

What is one good thing about your parents' relationship?

Question 560

Are you a cat person or a dog person? Why?

Question 561

What do you think are the ground rules for our relationship?

Question 562

How many children would you like?

Question 563

Do you enjoy foreplay or penetration more? Why? What excites you?

Question 564

Has there come a point in your life when you felt you couldn't go on? When? What happened?

Question 565

Would you still like me if we were not attracted to each other?

Question 566

What was your best holiday? Tell me about it?

Question 567

Do you feel isolated?

Question 568

Have you ever googled yourself? What did you find?

Question 569

Why is the divorce rate so high?

Question 570

Do you feel like you are struggling or thriving now?

Question 571

At what time of day do you have the most energy?

Question 572

Is there any way we can help stop modern slavery? Have you ever encountered someone you suspected was a slave or purchased something that seemed too cheap?

Question 573

Is there a brand that you consider yourself loyal to? Why?

Question 574

Does my family sometimes annoy you? What do they do?

Question 575

Where is the most interesting place you have visited?

Question 576

Is it ok for people to be friends with their old ex partner?

Question 577

Are you afraid of losing me?

Question 578

Which of us is the fastest walker?

Question 579

Do I show you I appreciate you often enough?

Question 580

What superpower do you secretly wish you had?

Question 581

Would you rather have take away delivered or pick it up yourself?

Question 582

Do you think it is important who is right when we have an argument? Does it matter if one person is right if the other person gets hurt?

Question 583

What is something that you pretended to like at the start of the relationship to make yourself more appealing to me?

Question 584

Should we have more foreplay? What is your favourite part?

Question 585

What would you do if you could spend a week with our bodies swapped?

Question 586

Are you more flexible and open now than you were five years ago or less?

Question 587

Which sex toys should we experiment with?

Question 588

Have you ever been jealous? What happened?

Question 589

Did your parents resolve their fights in front of you? How did they do it? How would you like to do it differently?

Question 590

What would you like to get ten thousand hours of experience in and why?

Question 591

Why do you think men have created so many inventions?

Question 592

What is your favourite city?

Question 593

Would you still want to live if you lost all your limbs?

Question 594

How does your period effect how you feel about sex? Do you still enjoy sex when you have your period?

Question 595

Has choosing me limited you in any way? How?

Question 596

What would we do if our child told us they were transgender?

Question 597

Should women stay with men who hurt them emotionally or physically?

Question 598

Would you be ok if we moved to a different country? Which one?

Question 599

What would you do if you thought I was leaving you?

Question 600

Has anyone ever asked you for help and you weren't able to help them? What happened?

Question 601

How did it feel when I first asked you out?

Question 602

Which aspect of your life is the best right now; work, family or friends?

Question 603

Do you have a favourite artist?

Question 604

Do you think most of your achievements have been accomplished by yourself or as a result of a lot of people supporting you?

Question 605

When was the lowest point in our relationship? How did we get through it?

Question 606

What colour eyes do each of your parents have?

Question 607

How long does it take you to calm down after being really upset?

Question 608

When has someone else been the most angry and upset with you? What happened?

Question 609

Will you kiss me now?

Question 610

If you were aquatic, what kind of animal, fish, reptile or vertebrae would you be?

Question 611

Which do you prefer, the beach or the snow?

Question 612

Is the air conditioning always too warm or too cold at work?

Question 613

How do you feel about refuges?

Question 614

In what ways are your friends similar?

Question 615

Should we turn more areas into National Parks?

Question 616

Does it matter if animals suffer? Should we be vegetarians?

Question 617

Would you ever consider getting solar power and going off grid?

Question 618

On a scale of one to ten, how has your day been? How can I increase it by one point?

Question 619

What has been our greatest single expense this year?

Question 620

Do you feel like you are achieving a lot?

Question 621

When have you been most relieved? What happened?

Question 622

Do you apologise for things that are not your fault?

Question 623

How could I improve my timing?

Question 624

Do you think love is sometimes a weakness? When?

Question 625

Could we do more to help people who are less fortunate than we are together? Do you want to?

Question 626

How do you feel about spiders and snakes?

Question 627

Has something psychic ever happened to you?

Question 628

Do you think most people have an origin story they tell themselves? What is yours?

Question 629

What do you think happens when you sleep? How do you experience it?

Question 630

Do you feel lucky?

Question 631

Who cleans the bathroom? Should the other person clean it more often?

Question 632

Are you a gardener? What would you like to grow?

Question 633

Do I make you feel safe?

Question 634

What is the sexiest thing I've ever worn?

Question 635

Do you feel rejected when I'm too tired to make love?

Question 636

Are you always over prepared or under prepared?

Question 637

What kind of sheets do you like to sleep on?

Question 638

Do you find it easy to say no to sex when you are too tired? Can we
have a signal or safe word for that so that sex continues to be
something we both enjoy?

Question 639

What is the best night's sleep you've ever had?

Question 640

Do you feel comfortable being without your phone? How long do
you think you could go without it?

Question 641

What are the top three best days of your life?

Question 642

Should we bring back extinct species? Which ones?

Question 643

Do you think inequality is a problem?

Question 644

When have you been most vulnerable? Tell me about it, what was it like? How did other people treat you?

Question 645

What is the most expensive thing you have ever damaged or broken?

Question 646

Can you change a flat tyre? Can you check tyre pressure?

Question 647

Do you ever feel like sex and then get too tired waiting for me to come to bed so you go to sleep instead?

Question 648

Do you avoid conflict if possible?

Question 649

Is it ok to let a baby cry for a while?

Question 650

Do you prefer being inside or outside?

Question 651

Is it ok to see each other go to the toilet or does it ruin the

romance?

Question 652

Do you prefer real soap or liquid soap?

Question 653

Is it better to be funny or smart?

Question 654

Would we ever have a relative live with us and would we care for

them?

Question 655

Do you feel like you get sick more often than other people or less?

Question 656

Which of us is better at baking cakes?

Question 657

Do you think I care about my appearance enough?

Question 658

If we had a baby would you let them use a dummy?

Question 659

Is it important to be assertive?

Question 660

Do you think older people should sacrifice for younger people?

Question 661

What time would you like to eat at night?

Question 662

Is it sexy when I bend over to do something?

Question 663

Can you remember your first teacher at school? What were they

like?

Question 664

Do you think it's important to be ruthless in business?

Question 665

What do you think will be your best legacy?

Question 666-777

Question 666

Do you think we live in a meritocracy?

Question 667

If you could make one wish for the world, what would it be?

Question 668

Do you think people should be able to do whatever they want so long as they don't hurt other people?

Question 669

Do you ever find it difficult to sleep?

Question 670

What is your most glorious memory?

Question 671

Does sex become physically less enjoyable if we do it too often? Is it more enjoyable after a break?

Question 672

Do you believe in prayer?

Question 673

What is your favourite foreign food?

Question 674

Are there any activities you enjoy doing more with other people?

Question 675

What do you want to do with your life?

Question 676

How important is it for us to be friends?

Question 677

Do you feel like you are contributing enough to the family financially?

Question 678

What is the one thing you want to be for other people?

Question 679

Is there any food that disgusts you?

Question 680

What sport or exercise would you like to spend more time doing?

How can I help you do it?

Question 681

What is one habit you would like to change?

Question 682

Do you enjoy doing things more in the morning or night?

Question 683

Which of my clothes would you like to give away?

Question 684

What do I do that makes you want to touch me?

Question 685

Do you find it hard to ask for help?

Question 686

What is your favourite drink?

Question 687

Do you prefer swimming, walking, running, riding a horse or bike riding?

Question 688

Did you enjoy school? Why or why not?

Question 689

What are three things on your bucket list you would like to do in the next five years?

Question 690

In business is it a zero sum game or do you want a fair outcome for everyone?

Question 691

What does music mean to you?

Question 692

Are miracles real – have you ever had one happen to you?

Question 693

What is your favourite tree?

Question 694

Do you wish you knew more names of birds and plants?

Question 695

What does your family think about me?

Question 696

Have you ever thought about suicide? What helps you overcome

these thoughts?

Question 697

Do you think the pay disparity between men and women is fair?

Question 698

What is the most unwell you have ever been?

Question 699

Has your mum ever talked about your birth? What was it like?

Question 700

Are you good at keeping secrets? How confidential is anything that

I tell you?

Question 701

When is the last time I wrote you a love letter, how did it make you

feel?

Question 702

Have you ever looked at an animal or fish or octopus and thought

they were looking back?

Question 703

Is it better to be brutally honest or to tell white lies and be kind?

Question 704

Are you competitive? Is it a good or a bad thing most of the time?

Question 705

Who looked after you when you were sick as a child?

Question 706

How did you feel after the first time we had sex?

Question 707

Should humans alter our genes to make ourselves more resistant to disease? Would you want our children to have this gene editing done?

Question 708

What is the best thing I have ever done for you?

Question 709

How do you feel when I touch you?

Question 710

What is a secret aspiration that you have never told anyone about before?

Question 711

What are five good things you have done with your life?

Question 712

When was the last time you felt frustrated with me, what

happened?

Question 713

Do you enjoy spooning together?

Question 714

How would you feel if I kissed someone of a different sex to you?

Question 715

Do we need to have more separate friends?

Question 716

Would you rather draw, talk or read?

Question 717

Do you enjoy giving oral sex?

Question 718

Is there music or a movie we can watch that helps you want to be intimate?

Question 719

When was the last time you felt excited about something? What was it?

Question 720

Is it ok for a wife to be more financially successful than her husband?

Question 721

What is your favourite savoury food?

Question 722

Are you comfortable being naked in front of other people?

Question 723

How do you react to constructive criticism?

Question 724

If you could time travel when and where would you go?

Question 725

When have I touched you most tenderly?

Question 726

Are there positions in sex you would like to try, which ones?

Question 727

Do you need to feel connected to have sex?

Question 728

What would it take to stop climate change?

Question 729

Did you have a teacher who really influenced you at school?

Question 730

What is your favourite movie of all time?

Question 731

When did you last feel stressed about money, why?

Question 732

Do you enjoy going to parties? Should we be more or less social?

Question 733

When do you find yourself behaving like your mother or father,

how would you like to change?

Question 734

What first attracted you to me?

Question 735

Would you stay if we couldn't have sex?

Question 736

Do you think we have free will?

Question 737

What is the oddest thing that you do? What is the oddest thing that I do?

Question 738

Is politics important to you?

Question 739

How have we changed since we first met?

Question 740

Is there anything I wear that makes me less attractive to you?

Question 741

What do we need to do to make our relationship work in the long term?

Question 742

Do you prefer day or night?

Question 743

How can I help you if your parents lose their facilities?

Question 744

When did you last have an argument with a friend? How did you resolve it?

Question 745

Are you addicted to anything?

Question 746

What is your favourite form of foreplay?

Question 747

Do you feel you are getting enough respect from your parents, children, friends and colleagues?

Question 748

What is the most inspiring movie you have ever watched?

Question 749

If one of us gave birth, would you like the other person to be in the room?

Question 750

When have you grown the most as a person?

Question 751

Do you enjoy your work? Is it time to make a change of work or career?

Question 752

What would you like to be like when you are in your seventies?

Question 753

Should we make more of our furniture around the house?

Question 754

Do you enjoy racy novels or porn? Would you like us to enjoy them together or separately, do you think it is wrong to enjoy them by ourselves?

Question 755

What would you like to achieve in the next year?

Question 756

Do you like to swear? Would you like to swear less?

Question 757

What is your favourite memory of sex with us?

Question 758

Should we spend more time gardening?

Question 759

What is your favourite part of your own body?

Question 760

How can we have better relationships with friends?

Question 761

Who does most of the talking in our relationship?

Question 762

Do you like it when I give you flowers? Would you prefer something else?

Question 763

Is emotional cheating equivalent to physically cheating?

Question 764

The different genders can do many different things, what do you most envy about the opposite sex?

Question 765

What is the most important thing in our life right now?

Question 766

Does any part of your body ache or hurt right now? Can I help with a massage?

Question 767

What is one thing you would like to do more of together?

Question 768

Can you name five things I do that you love?

Question 769

Do you need sex to help us feel connected?

Question 770

What is the best thing I have ever given you?

Question 771

Should we get rid of all the nuclear weapons in the world?

Question 772

Where is the most unusual place we have made love?

Question 773

Should we schedule a day and time to have sex?

Question 774

Do you have a favourite number?

Question 775

Is there someone in our lives that needs help right now? How can we help them?

Question 776

What have you learned about yourself from the different places you have lived?

Question 777-888

Question 777

Can you name the three most romantic things that I have done for you?

Question 778

What are some of the things we enjoy doing together?

Question 779

How are we different? Are you attracted to our similarities or our differences?

Question 780

What do you think about when you miss me?

Question 781

Would we survive being apart for eight months? How long could we survive without each other?

Question 782

What are three things you do that you don't want our kids to do?

Question 783

Are we stronger when we spend time apart? Would we be stronger

by ourselves?

Question 784

What is one preconceived idea you had about yourself that has

changed since we've been together?

Question 785

Why do you think we fell so hard for each other?

Question 786

What are two things we are doing really well to keep our

relationship thriving?

Question 787

Are you making a positive difference in the world?

Question 788

What is the best party you have ever been to?

Question 789

Have you ever wanted to write a novel? What would it be about?

Question 790

How would you like to die? Would you like to die at home, or would you go to the hospital to gain every last second of life?

Question 791

What excites you about growing old together, what scares you?

Question 792

Do you enjoy receiving oral sex?

Question 793

Which of us is the worst driver? Which of us is the worst backseat driver?

Question 794

Do you consider yourself to be a nerd? Why or why not?

Question 795

What were your favourite subjects at school?

Question 796

Do you prefer relaxing in the pool or curling up next to a fire?

Question 797

What are you afraid will happen in our relationship?

Question 798

How important is honesty in a relationship? How can I be more honest with myself and you?

Question 799

Did your parents have any miscarriages that you know about when you were growing up?

Question 800

How would you like our ideal home to look and feel?

Question 801

Which journey have you been on that really changed how you saw
the world?

Question 802

Do you think people are fundamentally good?

Question 803

If you could, would you want the male partner to breastfeed the
baby as well?

Question 804

Have you ever resigned? Why?

Question 805

When would we be too old to be parents for the first time?

Question 806

How were you different five years ago? How were you different ten years ago?

Question 807

Is there something I do when we're making love that really excites you?

Question 808

What are you most passionate about?

Question 809

Do I use social media too much or too little?

Question 810

Can you remember a time we compromised on something? Was it fair?

Question 811

Have you ever experienced butterflies in your stomach?

Question 812

Do you think women should be able to take their shirt off in public like men do?

Question 813

How much is it ok for me to tell people about us? What would you like to be kept private?

Question 814

Would we ever put a gps tracker on our kids?

Question 815

Do you enjoy hugging?

Question 816

Where did you see the most spectacular sunrise that you have ever seen?

Question 817

Are you sometimes timid? What gives you the strength to break out of your shell?

Question 818

Do you sing in the shower or in the car?

Question 819

Would you be ok if I didn't breastfeed so that we would be more

equal as parents and could both feed the baby?

Question 820

How many pets would you like? What would they be?

Question 821

Do you sometimes dread me coming home? Why and when?

Question 822

What is the trashiest thing I do?

Question 823

Do you prefer tea, coffee or hot chocolate?

Question 824

How do you feel about secondhand things?

Question 825

Should we think about the ways we could receive passive income?

Question 826

Do you get hangry? What are the signs?

Question 827

What is your favourite metal or stone?

Question 828

Do you prefer an older style of building or a newer one?

Question 829

What would you do if we lost all our financial assets overnight?

Question 830

Do you think it's healthy for you to be my best friend or should we have other close relationships to support us as well?

Question 831

What are three things you cannot live without?

Question 832

Do you find cooking sexy?

Question 833

Which areas am I better at leading in and which areas should I follow your lead in?

Question 834

Would you ever consider adoption? How would we help the adopted kids stay connected with a different cultural heritage?

Question 835

Do you have a favourite perfume?

Question 836

How would you feel if you quit your job yesterday?

Question 837

What name would you like to give a pet? Why?

Question 838

Do you know first aid? Is it something we should know?

Question 839

If we had a dog do you think it would start to look like us? Which

of us would it resemble more?

Question 840

How has your hometown shaped who you are?

Question 841

Do you have a favourite tree?

Question 842

Are you comfortable being naked in front of me?

Question 843

Is it important to know about popular culture or high culture?

Question 844

When is less more? When is more more?

Question 845

Do you enjoy where we live? What is great and what could be better?

Question 846

What is your dream car?

Question 847

Do you prefer books, tv or movies?

Question 848

Would we name our kids after relatives? Which ones?

Question 849

Do you believe in something controversial? What is it and why?

Question 850

Are you afraid of public speaking?

Question 851

What is your favourite place to visit right now?

Question 852

If you could be any aquatic creature what would it be?

Question 853

What do you think of tattoos? Have you got any, would you ever?

Question 854

Do you enjoy working hard?

Question 855

How are you feeling physically right now?

Question 856

Which room in your home is your favourite? Why?

Question 857

Did you keep a dairy when you were younger? What do you think of what you wrote then?

Question 858

What is the best thing that has happened this week?

Question 859

Should one of us be the head of the household?

Question 860

What does beauty mean to you?

Question 861

What is your favourite cartoon character?

Question 862

Is it ok if I track where you are on your phone if you're running late? Or is it too much like stalking?

Question 863

How do you feel about dinosaurs?

Question 864

Where did you see the most glorious rainbow you have ever seen?

Question 865

Would you still love me if I was bald?

Question 866

Can you whistle?

Question 867

What boundaries are important to you?

Question 868

Is money a sign of value sometimes?

Question 869

Have you ever been naked in a public place?

Question 870

What will we do when the kids are sick and we are too? Would we

take turns to care for them to give each of us a chance to get better?

Question 870

Do you prefer listening to music through EarPods, in the car, by a

speaker in the house or from a record player?

Question 871

Do you talk about sex with your friends?

Question 872

How can we really cherish and appreciate each other without taking

anything for granted?

Question 873

Do you feel better when you see a large open horizon like the

ocean?

Question 874

Is it ok for women to breastfeed in public?

Question 875

Are you tired? How can we feel refreshed?

Question 876

Have I ever ignored your advice and it has made you frustrated?

What happened?

Question 877

Do you enjoy gossip?

Question 878

Are you afraid of the dark sometimes? When?

Question 879

What is the longest time you have been stuck somewhere? What happened?

Question 880

Would you ever want to be fully self-sustainable, growing your own food and raising your own animals?

Question 881

If you could learn any musical instrument, what would it be?

Question 882

Could you swim in the ocean at night?

Question 883

Do you swear? What do you say?

Question 884

When is a time in your life that you have been incredibly bold?

What happened?

Question 885

How would you be a different parent than your parents?

Question 886

How important are birthday cards?

Question 887

If you could be any creature that flies what would you be?

Question 888

If I had to complete a quest to win your heart, what would it be?

Congratulations!

That was a marathon, you love each other enough to answer 888 questions, very impressive.

It is a sign that you are committed to growing and strengthening your relationship. Take a moment to stare into each other's eyes and dwell on how incredible your partner is and how incredibly lucky you both are.

We hope that you really enjoyed thinking about these questions and that they have stimulated deeper conversations. It takes courage to be vulnerable enough to share yourself in this way. We hope that by asking these questions that you have fallen even more deeply in love. Because being in love creates people who enjoy living and give back to the world around them.

The time we live in is extraordinary in that we have the potential to have the best relationships in human history. Not only can women choose their partners for the first time, men can share their burdens and have equal, fulfilling relationships. People can identify as who they truly are. This is incredible and worth celebrating. You may be at a place in your life right now when you realise it is the strong bonds and relationships we have in our lives that really matter and you have committed a significant amount of time to strengthening your relationship. You are both generous, caring partners who cherish what your partner thinks and feels.

Congratulations again on this extraordinary achievement.

9 798378 778560